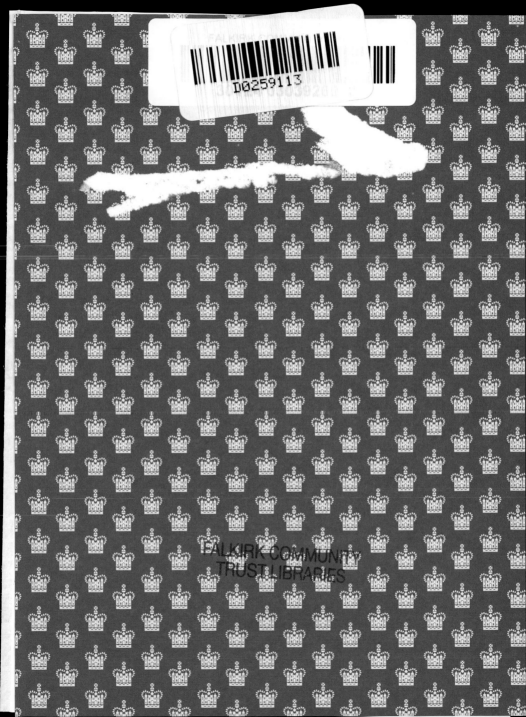

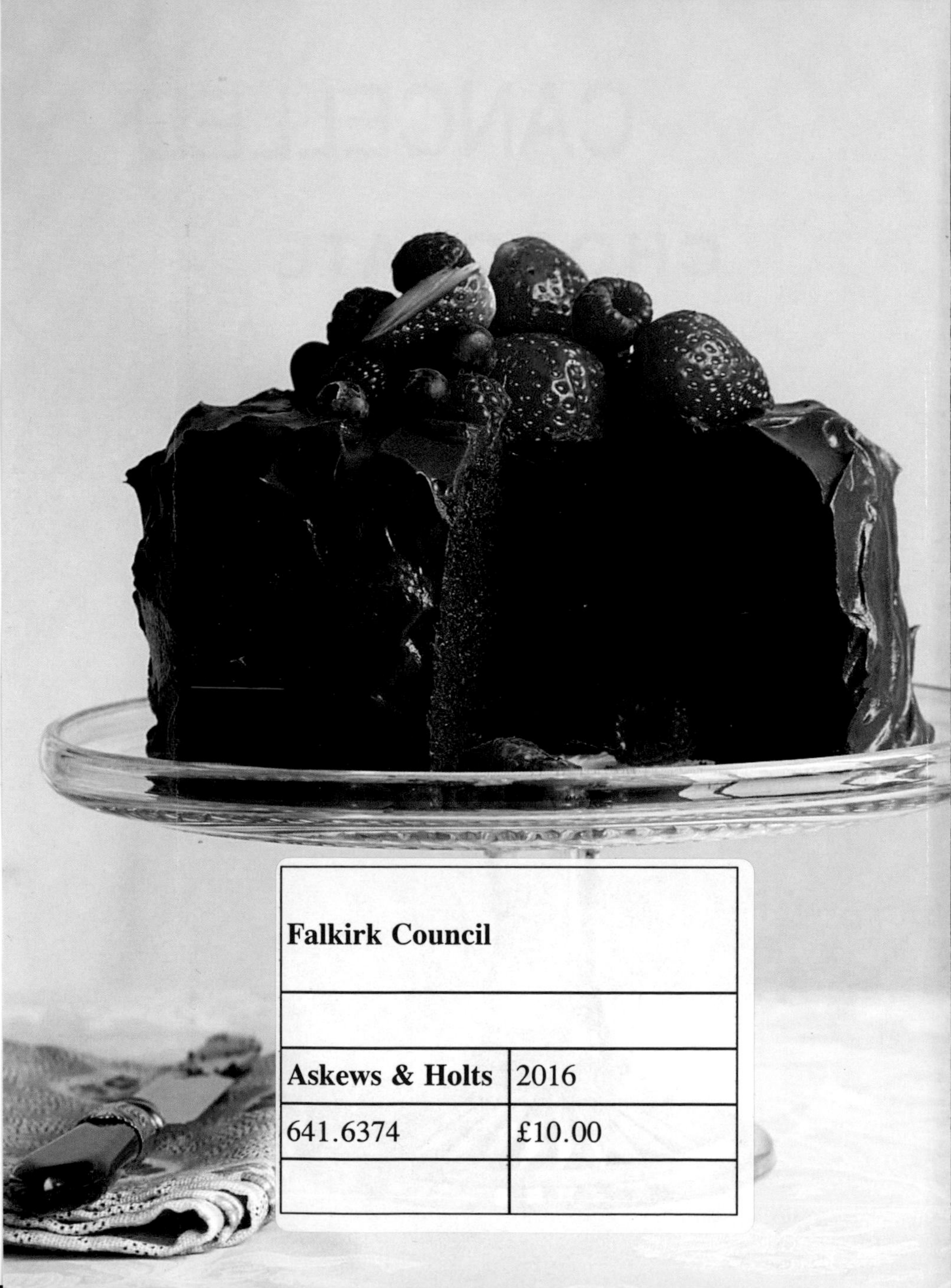

CHOCOLATE
FIT FOR A
QUEEN

❖ DELECTABLE CHOCOLATE RECIPES ❖

In association with
HISTORIC ROYAL PALACES

EBURY
PRESS

CONTENTS

Picture left and next page: Hampton Court Palace

INTRODUCTION
BY LUCY WORSLEY
CHIEF CURATOR OF
HISTORIC ROYAL
PALACES

The Countess of Winchelsea was ill. Her malady was her grief following the death of her husband, and in the seventeenth century this was recognised as an illness. You could literally die 'of melancholy' and it is recorded as a cause of death in bills of mortality.

But luckily the Countess's doctor, Sir Hans Sloane, had a cure, and the medicine he prescribed was chocolate.

Today we no longer believe that chocolate can cure a broken heart; we think it more likely to injure you – through a heart attack. Yet everyone can recognise its comforting, warming, enlivening qualities, whether eaten or drunk. And some of its qualities remain the same: the Stuarts and Georgians served chocolate to their courtiers as a treat, to thank them for coming to court and for serving the monarch, just as today, if someone looks after your pet while you're away, you're more likely than not to buy them a box of chocs.

But chocolate to the Countess of Winchelsea would have been a drink rather than a food: something rather like our hot chocolate but with added extras such as port wine or egg. Chocolate in Britain initially became popular at the court of Charles II, whose accounts include payments to a servant 'for grinding Cococ Nuts'. He also favoured chocolate flavoured with exotic ingredients, like ambergris (from sperm whales) and civet (from the glands of an African cat). Charles II was following the fashion of the Spanish royal family who had good access to the 'Cococ Nuts' of their conquered Mayan and Aztec subjects in Central America.

Among Charles II's successors, Queen Anne was such an enthusiastic chocolate drinker that she consumed 90 pint-pots of chocolate each month – although one hopes that her ladies-in-waiting helped her out. However, we are talking about the queen sometimes referred to disrespectfully as 'Square-Coffin'. Because of her great weight at death, her coffin had to be carried by 12 Yeomen of the Guard.

The history sections of this book have been brilliantly written by Polly Putnam, one of our curators at Historic Royal Palaces, who was tasked with researching the history of the fantastically interesting 'Chocolate Kitchen' at Hampton Court. Built for King William III and Queen Mary II in around 1691, these rooms were re-opened to our visitors in 2014, and in them you can learn the full story of how chocolate was prepared and drunk at court.

After spending a couple of years in this odd corner of the past, Polly can legitimately claim to be among the world's very few experts in the history of chocolate. I'm sure you'll find her insights a treat.

Lucy Worsley

CAKES

PLUM AND WHITE CHOCOLATE CAKE

Victoria plums were named after the much-loved nineteenth-century monarch after they were discovered in a garden in Sussex the year she was crowned. Juicy and sweet, they are Britain's most popular variety of plum and are delicious when used in baking. Here, the vibrant purple fruits are allowed to shine, keeping this simple cake deliciously moist and light; the white chocolate plays second fiddle, adding just a subtle hint of sweetness.

Serves 16

200g unsalted butter, softened, plus extra to grease

175g golden caster sugar

3 medium eggs, at room temperature, beaten

25g plain flour

200g self-raising flour

½ tsp baking powder

1 tsp vanilla extract

25g ground almonds

50g white chocolate, finely chopped

50–75ml milk

8 plums

To serve

2–3 tbsp apricot conserve

juice of ½ orange

Preheat the oven to 190°C/fan 170°C/gas 5. Grease and line a 20cm round cake tin with greaseproof paper.

Beat the butter and sugar together in a large bowl until the mixture is pale and creamy. Gradually add the eggs, beating all the time. If the mixture looks as if it might curdle, whisk in a spoonful of plain flour.

Sift over the two types of flour and baking powder, then add the vanilla extract, ground almonds, white chocolate and some of the milk. Fold everything together with a large metal spoon. If the mixture is very thick, add a splash more milk.

Set two plums aside. Halve the remaining six plums, remove the stones and roughly chop. Fold into the cake mixture then spoon the mixture into the tin.

Halve the remaining plums, then slice each half into three pieces. Lay them on top of the cake mixture but don't press them in. Bake in the oven for around 1 hour 15 minutes until the cake is golden and cooked through – the plums will gradually sink into the top of the cake as the sponge bakes and rises. Test the cake by pushing a metal skewer into the centre – it should come out clean. Take the cake out of the tin and transfer to a wire rack to cool.

To serve, put the apricot conserve into a pan with the orange juice. Bring to a simmer for 1–2 minutes until thickened. Strain into a bowl.

Carefully lift the cake on to a cake plate and serve sliced with the apricot sauce drizzled over the top of each slice.

CHOCOLATE ORANGE MADELEINES

The history of these buttery little French cakes is a little clouded but it is thought that they were originally served to French royalty in the eighteenth century. King Stanislaus of Lorraine got himself into a sticky situation when his pastry chef abandoned preparations for a lavish banquet he was hosting. His faithful maid Madeleine came to the rescue, baking a recipe belonging to her grandmother, and so delighted was the king with the result that he named the cakes after her. We've added a citrusy twist to the original recipe, and dipped them in melted chocolate; a picture-perfect finish fit for a king.

Makes 12

75g unsalted butter, plus extra to grease

75g self-raising flour, plus extra to dust

75g golden caster sugar

2 medium eggs, at room temperature

½ level tsp baking powder

grated zest of 1 orange

To decorate

50g milk chocolate

Preheat the oven to 210°C/fan 190°C/gas 7. Grease the moulds of a 12-hole madeleine tray, then dust generously with flour.

Melt the butter in a pan and put to one side to cool.

Whisk the sugar and eggs together in a bowl until the mixture is moussey and leaves a ribbon-like trail when the whisk is lifted. This will take 10–15 minutes if you use a hand whisk and around 5 minutes if you use a freestanding mixer.

Sift the flour and baking powder over the top of the bowl, then drizzle the cooled melted butter around the edge. Add the orange zest and fold everything together.

Divide the mixture evenly among the moulds and bake for around 8–10 minutes until golden. Use a palette knife to carefully lift each madeleine from the moulds and transfer to a wire rack to cool.

To decorate, melt the chocolate in a heatproof bowl set over a pan of simmering water, making sure the base of the bowl doesn't touch the water.

Once the chocolate has melted completely, dip the madeleines into it to coat each cake by about a third. Put on a tray lined with baking parchment and leave to set.

DARK CHOCOLATE SQUARES
WITH RASPBERRIES

The batter for this chocolate cake makes quite a firm sponge, which means that once it has cooled it's really easy to slice. It is perfect for cutting into neat little squares and serving as a sweet canapé at a party or buffet.

Makes 25

150g unsalted butter, chopped, plus extra to grease

200g dark chocolate (minimum 50 per cent cocoa solids), finely chopped

175g golden caster sugar

2 large eggs, at room temperature

175g self-raising flour

25g cocoa powder

To decorate

150ml double cream

1 tbsp icing sugar

25 raspberries

Preheat the oven to 190°C/fan 170°C/gas 5. Grease and line a 19cm square cake tin with baking parchment.

Melt the butter and 150g of the chocolate in a pan over a low heat. Carefully mix together then set aside to cool a little.

Whisk the sugar and eggs together in a bowl using an electric hand whisk until the mixture is moussey and falls in thick ribbons when the whisks are lifted.

Sift over the flour and cocoa powder then add the melted chocolate mixture along with the remaining chopped chocolate. Fold everything together carefully using a large metal spoon. Transfer the mixture to the tin and spread it evenly.

Bake in the oven for 30 minutes until firm. Cool in the tin for 10 minutes then transfer to a wire rack to cool completely.

To serve, whip the double cream with the icing sugar until just firm. Cut the cake into 25 squares and spoon a little whipped cream on top of each. Top each square with a raspberry.

FOOD OF THE GODS

Chocolate is one of the oldest luxury commodities and has been a source of pleasure and a demonstration of privilege for many cultures through the ages, from the ancient Mesoamericans to the European monarchy. The berries of the tree *Theobroma cacao* – whose name means 'food of the gods' – were eaten in Central America for thousands of years, and in Belize traces of chocolate have been found on the shards of spouted vessels that date back to 1100 BC.

Harvesting cacao is difficult as the Theobroma tree requires precise levels of humidity and exacting temperatures in order to bear fruit. The process of making chocolate is also skilled and time-consuming as the beans need to be left to ferment in their pods before they can be ground and roasted. Cacao beans were therefore much prized by the earliest Mesoamerican civilisations.

Chocolate was used as a currency throughout Central America – the Nicaro people of Nicaragua could buy a nice fat rabbit for four beans, while a slave cost 100 beans. Likewise Europeans in the sixteenth century remarked on the 'happie monie' that literally grew on trees.

Chocolate has been enjoyed in various forms since human beings discovered a taste for sweet things. Both the Mayans and Aztecs featured chocolate in their religion and their rituals. The Aztecs used chocolate made from muddy water to symbolise blood, which was poured over a young warrior's spear as part of an initiation ceremony.

The Lacandón Mayans created a chocolate drink as an offering to their gods, adding a special grass called 'aak' to make it extra foamy. In the Yucatán, Mayan children reaching puberty were anointed with a 'holy' mixture of ground cacao beans, flowers and water to mark and bless their passage into adulthood. Furthermore, during marriage ceremonies, beans were exchanged between husband and wife as a sign of their promise to each other.

For Mayans especially, chocolate was an essential part of celebrating and feasting; instead of breaking bread they drank chocolate. At a typical Mayan feast amongst noblemen, each guest was given a roasted fowl and a chocolate drink flavoured with peppers, chilli and aromatic flowers, which they drank in abundance. Mayans even had a specific verb meaning 'to drink chocolate together' – *Chokola'j* – from which the word chocolate derives.

From the sixteenth century the Spanish occupied areas of Central America, and among the plunder they brought back to Europe were Mayan and Aztec recipes for preparing chocolate with sugar and spices. The Spanish also passed on the culture and rituals surrounding chocolate drinking, and royal European families began to associate chocolate with luxury, sociability and gift-giving.

CHOCOLATE MUFFINS

The key to making really light muffins is to stir the wet and dry ingredients together quickly. You only need a very light touch and should still be able to see bits of flour when you stop mixing. If you overmix and make a smooth batter your muffins will be dense and heavy.

Makes 6

200g self-raising flour

1 tsp baking powder

40g cocoa powder

40g dark chocolate (minimum 60 per cent cocoa solids), roughly chopped

50g unsalted butter, melted and cooled

175g natural yoghurt

75-100ml milk

1 medium egg, at room temperature

100g golden caster sugar

Preheat the oven to 200°C/fan 180°C/gas 6. Line a six-hole muffin tray with paper cases.

Sift the flour, baking powder and cocoa powder into a bowl and stir in the dark chocolate.

In a separate bowl, whisk together the butter, yoghurt, milk, egg and sugar. Pour this on to the dry mixture and very roughly fold everything together, taking care not to overmix. Don't worry if there are a few dry patches in the mix, they'll cook through, and by stirring everything together quickly the muffins will be lovely and light.

Divide the mixture among the paper cases and bake for 25-30 minutes until a skewer inserted into the centre comes out clean. Transfer to a wire rack to cool, then serve.

CHOCOLATE FRIDGE CAKE

There are many variations of this crunchy chocolatey offering, which is so simple to make because it is set in the fridge rather than being baked. Our recipe is based on the version thought to be Prince William's favourite childhood treat. So great is his fondness for fridge cake that at his wedding the prince revived a great Victorian tradition and requested to have a 'groom's cake' alongside the traditional fruit cake.

Serves 12

150g unsalted butter, plus extra to grease

100g golden syrup

300g dark chocolate (minimum 50 per cent cocoa solids), chopped

1 tbsp brandy

200g Rich Tea or digestive biscuits

Grease and line a deep 16cm round cake tin with baking parchment.

Melt the butter in a pan with the syrup and 125g of the chocolate. As soon as all the ingredients have melted, stir in the brandy. Heat for 1 minute, then take the pan off the heat.

Use a large chopping knife to crush the biscuits, in batches, into bite-sized chunks. Make sure they're not too big otherwise the chocolate mixture won't coat the biscuits properly, or too small, which will make the texture dense.

Stir the biscuits into the chocolate mixture, ensuring they're all coated. Spoon into the lined tin, making sure there aren't any holes. Chill in the fridge for 1 hour or until firm.

Remove the cake from the tin and place on a rack, resting over a tray lined with baking parchment. Melt the remaining chocolate in a heatproof bowl set over a pan of simmering water, making sure the base of the bowl doesn't touch the water. Allow to cool for 10 minutes, then spoon all over the cake, ensuring the sides are covered. Cool at room temperature, then serve in thin slices. Store in an airtight container for up to five days.

DARK CHOCOLATE AND GINGER LOAF CAKE

The fiery notes of ginger are a perfect antidote to the richness of the chocolate in this sumptuous loaf cake. Ground ginger lends the chocolate sponge a subtle, spicy warmth while a topping of sugary crystallised ginger adds a sweet crunchy finish.

Makes 1 loaf, serves 8-10

40g dark chocolate (minimum 60 per cent cocoa solids), broken into pieces

40g crystallised ginger

125g unsalted butter, softened

125g light soft brown sugar

2 medium eggs, at room temperature, beaten

100g self-raising flour

45g cocoa powder

2 tsp ground ginger

75ml milk

To decorate

60g dark chocolate (minimum 60 per cent cocoa solids)

75ml double cream

10g crystallised ginger, chopped

Preheat the oven to 180°C/fan 160°C/gas 4. Line a 450g loaf tin with a paper cake liner.

Put the chocolate and crystallised ginger in a small food processor and whizz until finely chopped.

Beat the butter and sugar together in a bowl until the mixture is soft and creamy. Gradually beat in the eggs, then fold in the flour, cocoa powder, ground ginger and milk until smooth.

Spoon the mixture into the lined loaf tin and bake for around 50 minutes, until a skewer inserted into the centre comes out clean. Lift out of the tin and allow to cool on a wire rack.

To decorate, melt the chocolate in a heatproof bowl set over a pan of simmering water, making sure the base of the bowl doesn't touch the water. Stir in the double cream carefully to make a smooth ganache.

Spoon the ganache on top of the cake and scatter over the crystallised ginger, then leave to set before serving.

BLOOD VELVET CAKE

When 'Colonel' Thomas Blood tried to steal the Crown Jewels in 1671, the Tower of London was almost divested of its most precious treasures. Fortunately, his attempt was thwarted and the Tower's happy triumph over the thief is still commemorated there today with this chocolate-flavoured, blood-red-coloured cake. It's finished with a cream cheese icing and a nod to the historic event – chocolate crowns.

———————————— 👑 ————————————

Serves 10

100g unsalted butter, softened, plus extra to grease

250g golden caster sugar

2 large eggs, at room temperature, beaten

175g plain flour

25g cocoa powder, plus extra to dust

100ml buttermilk

½ tsp bicarbonate of soda

½ tbsp red wine vinegar

1½ tbsp edible red food colouring paste

For the chocolate crowns and icing

50g dark chocolate (minimum 50 per cent cocoa solids), broken into pieces

75g unsalted butter, softened

125g icing sugar

250g cream cheese

Preheat the oven to 180°C/fan 160°C/gas 4.

Grease and line a deep 16cm round cake tin with greaseproof paper. Whisk together the butter and sugar in a large bowl until soft and creamy. Gradually whisk in the eggs, adding a spoonful of flour if the mixture looks as if it's curdling. Sift over the remaining flour and cocoa powder.

In a separate bowl, mix the buttermilk, bicarbonate of soda, vinegar and food colouring paste together. Add to the flour mixture and fold everything together. Spoon into the tin and bake in the oven for 1 hour 10 minutes, or until a skewer inserted into the centre comes out clean. Remove from the tin and leave to cool on a wire rack.

For the chocolate crowns, put the chocolate into a heatproof bowl set over a pan of simmering water, making sure the base of the bowl doesn't touch the water. As soon as all the chocolate has melted, allow to cool for 5 minutes.

Cover a baking sheet with baking parchment. Spoon the chocolate into a small plastic bag, snip the very tip of one of the bag's bottom corners and pipe the shape of crowns by outlining three loops together, a bar underneath and a dot on top of the middle loop for a 'jewel'. Pipe more crowns than you need so you can choose the best shapes. Leave to set at room temperature.

For the icing, beat the butter and icing sugar together, then fold in the cream cheese until smooth. Carefully peel away the paper from the cake and place the cake on a serving plate. Put two large tablespoons of icing aside, then spoon one tablespoon on top of the cake. Smooth it over to cover, then work the mixture around the sides of the cake. Spoon the remaining mixture into a piping bag fitted with a star nozzle and pipe three swirls in the centre of the cake. Push a chocolate crown into each and serve.

BELGIAN CHOCOLATE CAKE

There's no doubt that chocolate is a favourite ingredient in today's royal household. Both Prince William and his grandmother are partial to a slice of Chocolate Fridge Cake (see page 25), while in 2006 Prince Charles hosted a surprise celebration for his mother's 80th birthday at which guests enjoyed a simple English menu followed by a sumptuous slice of chocolate sponge layered with a Highgrove fruit filling. While you won't be able to pick Highgrove's berries to make this cake, it is every bit as rich and decadent as its inspiration.

Serves 16

100g Belgian milk chocolate

a little unsalted butter, to grease

225g self-raising flour

1 tsp bicarbonate of soda

25g cocoa powder

125ml sunflower oil

75ml water

125g light soft brown sugar

2 medium eggs, at room temperature

For the filling and decoration

150g Belgian dark chocolate (minimum 70 per cent cocoa solids)

50ml milk

125ml double cream

2–3 tbsp raspberry jam

150g mixed summer fruit (strawberries, raspberries and blueberries)

Break the chocolate into pieces and put in a heatproof bowl set over a pan of just-simmering water, making sure the base of the bowl doesn't touch the water. Allow the chocolate to melt very slowly over this gentle heat. Once all the chocolate has melted, take the bowl off the pan and set aside to cool for 10 minutes.

Preheat the oven to 180°C/fan 160°C/gas 4. Grease and line two 20cm round cake tins with greaseproof paper.

Sift the flour, bicarbonate of soda and cocoa powder into a large bowl and make a well in the middle.

Stir the oil, water and sugar into the melted chocolate, then whisk in the eggs. Pour half the mixture into the well and fold in, then add the remaining chocolate mixture and mix well.

Divide the mixture evenly between the cake tins and bake in the oven for 20–25 minutes until a skewer inserted into the centre comes out clean. Remove the cakes from the tins and cool on a wire rack.

For the decoration, make a chocolate ganache icing by melting the dark chocolate in a heatproof bowl set over a pan of simmering water, as before. Once the chocolate has melted, stir in the milk, then set aside to cool.

Picture previous page: Hillsborough Castle

Whip the cream in a separate bowl until thick and moussey. Use a large metal spoon to add one large spoonful of the cream to the chocolate mixture and fold in. Continue to gently fold in the remaining cream until smooth.

Put one cake half on a cake stand and cover the top with the jam. Place the other cake half on top. Spoon about half the ganache on top of the cake and slowly start to work it down the sides to cover the cake. Continue to add spoonfuls of ganache to the sides until it is all covered. Put the remaining ganache on top and swirl it around to make a pleasing pattern.

Pile the summer fruit into the middle of the cake, slice and serve.

CHOCOLATE COMES TO COURT

Chocolate first arrived in England in the early 1600s. There is evidence it was drunk in the court of King Charles I (r1625–1649) before it was condemned by Oliver Cromwell's Protectorate as being sinfully pleasurable. However, it is really during the reign of King Charles II (r1660–1685) that chocolate drinking became a major feature of English court life. Charles II's ambassadors in Spain, who returned much enthused by the practice of chocolate drinking they had encountered there, praised it to the king who encouraged it at the English court. Nobles in the court would sip chocolate in special drawing rooms as a way of demonstrating their conviviality and generosity, and in Spain, chocolate was considered magnificent and was offered as a regal gift, or '*regalo*'.

Lady Ann Fanshawe, who was married to the Spanish Ambassador and often present at the Spanish court in Madrid, witnessed the royal family consume chocolate nearly every day. She described a typical family meal: 'The King and Queen eat together twice a week in public with their children, the rest privately, and asunder. They eat often, with flesh to their breakfast, which is generally, to persons of quality, a partridge and bacon, or capon, or some such thing, ever roasted, much chocolate, and sweetmeats, and new-laid eggs, drinking water either cold with snow, or lemonade, or some such thing.'

Charles II's private accounts reveal that he splashed out what at the time were staggering amounts of money on chocolate: in February 1669 he paid nearly £230 for a 'Receipt [recipe] of Chocolatte'. He also spent £4 for 'vanilloes for Chocalate' and £5–8 to 'Mr Kitsons man for grinding Cococ Nuts'. By 1682, the king had appointed his own chocolate maker, Solomon de la Faya, to keep the court regularly supplied with chocolate.

By serving chocolate at court, Charles II demonstrated to the powerful courtiers and foreign dignitaries that the king had access to an exotic commodity that pointed to his nation's power across the globe. Most importantly for Charles II, a monarch newly restored after civil war, this emphasised regality.

Successive sovereigns continued to favour chocolate. Queen Mary II (r1689–1694) was fascinated by anything new and foreign, and she was drawn to the exotic nature of chocolate. Her husband King William III (r1689–1702) drank it every day, often with his closest friends and associates. They liked it enough to have dedicated chocolate kitchens built at Kensington Palace, Windsor Castle and Hampton Court (see pages 50-51).

Their successor Queen Anne's (r1702–1714) chocolate intake was particularly impressive: her private accounts suggest that she bought enough chocolate to make 90 pint pots a month! Despite her somewhat portly appearance, this was far more than personal consumption; she was clearly providing chocolate at court.

Both the Georgian kings that followed her, Georges I (r1714–1727) and II (r1727–1760), were under pressure from Parliament to cut court budgets, yet they continued to employ chocolate makers, both for their own enjoyment and to provide for lavish court entertainments. King George II had chocolate for breakfast every morning, while his wife Queen Caroline also drank chocolate with her daughters and liked nothing more than a good gossip with her friend, the politician and diarist John Hervey, over a cup of chocolate in her private apartments.

WHITE CHOCOLATE BUTTERFLY CAKES WITH A BLUEBERRY DRIZZLE

The mention of the words 'butterfly cakes' will have most adults in Britain sighing with nostalgia, remembering childhood birthday parties where these dainty little morsels were standard fare. A small round is cut from the top of each cake to make 'wings', which are held in place by a creamy buttery icing. Sweetened with a hint of white chocolate and finished with a colourful blueberry drizzle, our recipe is perfect for a children's party – though we can't guarantee there won't be a few grown-up takers too.

Makes 12
100g butter, softened
100g caster sugar
2 medium eggs, at room temperature
100g self-raising flour
20g white chocolate, finely grated
grated zest of 1 lemon

For the icing
40g butter, softened
125g icing sugar
40g cream cheese

For the blueberry drizzle
75g blueberries
20g honey
a squeeze of lemon juice

Preheat the oven to 190°C/fan 170°C/gas 5. Line a 12-hole shallow cake tray with 12 paper cases.

Beat the butter and sugar together in a bowl until the mixture looks soft and creamy and slightly paler in colour. Gradually beat in the eggs, adding a little flour if the mixture looks as if it might curdle. Fold in the rest of the flour, the white chocolate and lemon zest.

Spoon the mixture evenly among the paper cases and bake in the oven for around 15 minutes until risen and golden. Transfer to a wire rack to cool.

For the icing, beat the butter in a bowl until softened, then gradually beat in the icing sugar. Carefully fold in the cream cheese to mix everything together. Chill in the fridge for 30 minutes.

To make the drizzle, put the blueberries in a pan with the honey and lemon juice. Bring to the boil and simmer for 2–3 minutes until the mixture looks jammy. Spoon into a bowl and allow to cool.

Use a small sharp knife to carefully cut a round in the top of each cake, remove and set this piece aside. Spoon the icing into a piping bag fitted with a 1cm nozzle and pipe a swirl of it into the holes on each cake. Cut the spare pieces of sponge in half and stick either side of the icing. Spoon a little blueberry drizzle on top and serve.

WHITE CHOCOLATE AND RASPBERRY ANGEL CAKE

Angel cake is made with egg whites only, no yolks, so it is a wonderfully light cake with virtually no fat. During baking it develops a sugary, golden crust that hides a tender, almost chewy white crumb. This summery twist on the classic recipe has a hint of tart raspberry in the batter and a simple cream coating; perfect served with a cup of tea at a picnic on the lawn.

Serves 12

a little vegetable oil, to grease

175g caster sugar

75g plain flour, plus extra to dust

6 medium egg whites, at room temperature

1 tsp vanilla extract

¾ tsp cream of tartar

2 tbsp freeze-dried raspberry bits

To decorate

300ml double cream

1 tsp icing sugar

1 tbsp freeze-dried raspberry bits

25g white chocolate, grated

Preheat the oven to 190°C/fan 170°C/gas 5. Grease a 24cm ring cake tin well with oil.

Whizz the sugar in a food processor to make it even finer. Put half in a bowl and stir in the flour. Sift this mixture into a separate bowl – this helps to produce a lovely light sponge.

Put the egg whites, vanilla extract and cream of tartar into a large bowl and whisk gently, using a hand whisk, to mix everything together lightly. Increase the speed and continue to whisk, gradually adding in the remaining sugar, until the mixture leaves a ribbon-like trail when you lift the beaters. You can also do this in a freestanding mixer if you have one.

Sift over the sugar and flour mixture, then scatter the freeze-dried raspberry bits on top. Fold everything together until smooth.

Spoon the mixture into the tin and bake for 30–40 minutes until the mixture is golden and feels firm when you press it. Leave to cool in the tin upside down on a wire rack.

Once cool, use a palette knife to carefully tease the sponge away from the sides of the tin then shake it out on to the wire rack. Transfer to a serving plate.

To serve, whip the double cream in a bowl with the icing sugar. Spoon all over the cake, then scatter over the raspberry bits and white chocolate and serve.

PASTRIES
AND
TARTS

CLASSIC CHOCOLATE TART

Good-quality chocolate should specify the percentage of cocoa solids it contains. The higher the percentage, the stronger the chocolate flavour. For an intense cocoa hit, choose a chocolate with no less than 70 per cent cocoa solids. This tart is for chocolate purists: smooth dark chocolate is paired with cocoa powder, the most highly concentrated form of chocolate. It is delicious served in thin slivers with whipped cream.

Serves 16

For the pastry

170g plain flour

85g chilled unsalted butter, cubed

1 egg yolk, at room temperature

20g icing sugar

For the filling

75g dark chocolate (minimum 70 per cent cocoa solids)

75g golden caster sugar

125ml double cream

15g cocoa powder, plus extra to dust

½ tsp espresso powder

1 tsp vanilla extract

2 medium eggs, at room temperature

Sift the flour into a food processor then add the butter. Whizz together until the mixture resembles fine crumbs.

Mix the egg yolk with 2 teaspoons of water then add to the food processor with the icing sugar. Whizz briefly, just until the mixture starts to form a dough, then tip into a bowl and bring together with your hands. Shape into a disc and wrap in greaseproof paper. Chill in the fridge for 20 minutes.

Unwrap the dough and roll it out until it's about 2–3mm thick. Use to a line a 20cm shallow tart tin. Prick all over the base with a fork, then cover loosely and chill for another 20 minutes.

Preheat the oven to 170°C/fan 150°C/gas 3.

Line the pastry base with greaseproof paper and fill with baking beans. Cook in the oven for 15 minutes until the base feels dry to the touch. Reduce the oven temperature to 150°C/fan 130°C/gas 2.

To make the filling, break the chocolate into pieces and put in a heatproof bowl set over a pan of simmering water, making sure the water doesn't touch the base of the bowl. Allow to melt, then take off the heat and cool a little.

Carefully stir together the sugar, double cream, cocoa powder, espresso powder, vanilla extract and 25ml of warm water into the chocolate and mix until smooth, then gently fold in the eggs. Pour into the tin and bake for 30 minutes until set.

Remove from the tin and cool until just warm. Dust with cocoa powder before serving.

CHOCOLATE CIGARELLOS

During the early eighteenth century, the French courts started serving elaborate pyramids of sweetmeats and fruit, a demonstration of excess and wealth that was designed to impress courtiers and guests. The fashion eventually spread to England and became so ingrained that a hostess would be judged on the elaborateness of her sweetmeats. We think these delicate chocolate rolls would have been a fine addition to a groaning table of confections: crisp filo pastry encases a crunchy, nutty filling, mixed with rich chocolate and orange.

———————————— 👑 ————————————

Makes 16

100g dark chocolate (minimum 60 per cent cocoa solids)

75g milk chocolate

3 large egg yolks, at room temperature

100g pine nuts, toasted

grated zest of 1 orange

2 tbsp light soft brown sugar

4 sheets filo pastry

50g unsalted butter, melted and cooled

a little icing sugar, to dust

Preheat the oven to 200°C/fan 180°C/gas 6. Line two baking sheets with baking parchment.

Break both the chocolates into pieces and put in a small food processor. Add the egg yolks, pine nuts and orange zest and blitz to chop all the ingredients finely. Stir in the sugar.

Put one sheet of filo pastry on a board, keeping the other sheets covered with a damp tea towel, and cut down the middle to make two halves, then cut each piece in half again to make four rectangles. Divide the chocolate mixture into four, then put about a quarter of each portion on to each rectangle. The mixture should hold its shape enough for you to mould it into a rough sausage.

Lie the sausage along the shortest edge of pastry, then move the pastry round so the sausage is sitting horizontally at the top. Roll the pastry towards you, tucking the ends in as you go. Brush the ends with melted butter then brush the filo pastry all over again with more butter. Continue until you've used all the pastry, filling it all with the chocolate mixture. Place all the rolled cigarellos on to the parchment.

Bake in the oven for 20 minutes. Dust with icing sugar and serve warm with coffee.

CHOCOLATE CHOUX CROWNS

Choux pastry provides a deliciously light, thin, crisp casing and, unlike other pastry doughs, the wet batter can be stuffed into a piping bag to create all manner of shapes. Choux is traditionally used for éclairs, profiteroles and savoury puffs but here we've piped it into regal-inspired rings. Don't worry if your piping isn't picture-perfect – once you've got the icing and golden decorations on your crowns and have spooned in the chocolate-studded whipped cream, they'll be every bit as majestic as they are moreish.

Makes 8

25g unsalted butter

40g plain flour, sifted

1 medium egg, at room temperature, beaten

100ml double cream

1 tsp icing sugar

15g white chocolate, finely chopped

For the icing

25g golden icing sugar

edible gold balls

Preheat the oven to 220°C/fan 200°C/gas 7. Line a baking sheet with baking parchment and draw eight 5.5cm circles, spaced apart, on it, then turn it over.

Place the butter in a pan with 75ml of water. Heat gently to melt the butter, then bring to a rolling boil.

Put the flour on to a sheet of greaseproof paper and 'shoot' it into the side of the pan. Beat with a wooden spoon until it forms a ball. Cool a little.

Gradually add the egg, beating well between each addition, until the mixture looks smooth and glossy and drops easily from the spoon. Transfer to a piping bag fitted with a 1cm nozzle. Pipe around the outlined circles once, then pipe another layer on top.

Push down any points with a wet finger, then splash a little water over the parchment to help create steam in the oven. Bake for 15 minutes until the rings are golden and puffed up. Put a little hole in the side of each one and return to the oven for a minute or two to dry out the middle.

Cut each ring in half horizontally. Whip the cream and icing sugar in a bowl until moussey, then stir in the chocolate. Divide the mixture among the bottoms of the rings, and replace the top halves. Stir the icing sugar and 1–1½ teaspoons of cold water until smooth. Drizzle over each crown then decorate with the gold balls. Leave to set before serving.

CHOCOLATE AND PRUNE TWISTS

Squidgy and sticky yet not too sweet, prunes are a natural partner for chocolate but also for a tipple. In France, the Gascons soak them in Armagnac and serve them after dinner to round off a meal, while the Italians use them to infuse grappa. Here we've combined the three flavours and rolled them into a crisp chocolate pastry twist. They're delicious served with a strong coffee, or take the French lead and accompany them with a brandy or Armagnac for a sophisticated finish.

Makes 8

40g ready-to-eat dried prunes

15ml brandy

grated zest of ½ orange

½ x 320g ready-rolled all-butter puff pastry

20g milk chocolate, broken into pieces

To decorate

15g white chocolate

5g pistachio nuts, chopped

icing sugar, to dust

Preheat the oven to 210°C/fan 190°C/gas 7. Preheat a baking sheet.

Whizz the prunes, brandy and orange zest together in a mini food processor.

Unroll the puff pastry and, with the longest edge lying horizontally, cut down the middle of it vertically.

Spread the prune mixture over one half and scatter over the milk chocolate pieces. Put the other half of the puff pastry on top and gently press down. Cut into 8 fingers.

Twist each finger and transfer to the preheated baking sheet. Bake for 15–20 minutes, until puffed up and golden all over.

Melt the white chocolate very gently on the lowest heat setting in the microwave for 10-20 seconds and drizzle it over each twist. Scatter over the chopped pistachio nuts then dust with icing sugar just before serving.

THE CHOCOLATE KITCHENS AT HAMPTON COURT PALACE

King William III and Queen Mary II were particularly enthusiastic chocolate drinkers. By the 1690s, they had established kitchens for making and serving chocolate at the palaces in Windsor, Kensington and Hampton Court. The chocolate rooms at Hampton Court Palace were built within Fountain Court, part of the radical refurbishment of the eastern side of the palace by Sir Christopher Wren. But the project signified far more than the whims of chocoholic monarchs. The huge expense incurred in buying the precious beans and equipment, the employment of a chocolate maker and the deliberate placing of the chocolate kitchens in an elegant and highly visible part of the new palace all helped to assert the monarchs' munificence and majesty.

As well as creating sets of state and private apartments on the upper levels, Wren designed new rooms including a confectionery, for making sweets and candies, a spice office, where the expensive spices were prepared and stored, and a chocolate kitchen on the ground floor. At Hampton Court, the chocolate kitchen itself contained state-of-the-art equipment, including a smoke jack over the fireplace to help automated bean roasting, and a brazier – in effect a Georgian stove. The less attractive aspects of culinary activity, such as butchery, remained out of sight in the ancient Tudor palace, while the ground floor kitchens and offices all housed activities that would have been pleasant to watch and smelled wonderful! The aromas of caramelising fruits, spices and chocolate must have delighted the courtiers and important guests strolling around Fountain Court. For foreign visitors especially, the chocolate kitchens signalled that the English court had ready access to these luxury items, and thus acted as a visual and olfactory reminder of England's colonial and trading power.

By 1701, an additional room was appointed to William III's chocolate maker, right next to the king's staircase. This allowed for chocolate to be brought quickly as and when the king wanted it. This room still exists with its original shutters, suggesting that it was used for storing the valuable items used for serving chocolate. These would have included exquisitely-made silver chocolate pots, porcelain and delftware cups, and their silver chocolate frames, and delicate glass dishes used to serve sweetmeats along with the chocolate, particularly at breakfast time. In 2014, the chocolate kitchens were restored and re-opened to public view, so visitors to Hampton Court Palace can now enjoy seeing how these elegant rooms, with many original fittings including the stove, once looked.

CHOCOLATE, PECAN AND WALNUT TARTS

Replacing some of the flour with cocoa creates a rich yet not too cloying pastry that turns this tart into something really special. Not only does the dark brown case look very striking, here it's balanced with a tempting, pale, crunchy nut filling.

Makes 6

For the pastry

50g unsalted butter, softened

1 tbsp icing sugar

1 medium egg yolk, at room temperature

a pinch of salt

100g plain flour

10g cocoa powder

For the filling

3 tbsp light brown soft sugar

40g unsalted butter

75ml double cream

75g walnuts and pecan nuts (half and half), chopped

a pinch of salt

Put the butter, icing sugar, egg yolk and salt into a mini food processor with 2 tablespoons of cold water. Whizz to blitz everything together and make a paste. Add the flour and cocoa powder and whizz again until the mixture starts to form a dough.

Tip into a bowl and bring together with your hands to make a dough. If the mixture feels dry, wet your hands first. Wrap the dough in baking parchment and shape into a disc then chill for 20 minutes.

Cut the dough into six pieces and roll out thinly, then use to line six 6.5cm shallow tartlet tins. Chill again for 20 minutes.

Preheat the oven to 200°C/fan 180°C/gas 6. Preheat a baking sheet.

To make the filling, put the brown sugar into a frying pan with 1½ tablespoons of cold water and heat gently until the mixture starts to bubble. Add the butter and allow to melt, then stir in the double cream and bring to the boil. As soon as the mixture is bubbling, stir in the nuts and salt and take off the heat.

Spoon the filling evenly among the tart tins and bake for 10 minutes, then turn the oven down to 150°C/fan 130°C/gas 2 and continue to bake for 15 minutes until the tarts are golden and cooked through. The mixture will be bubbling when you take it out of the oven, so leave the tarts to cool in the tins until just warm, then turn out and serve with a spoonful of thick cream.

Picture left: Hampton Court Palace

BLACKBERRY AND APPLE WHITE CHOCOLATE MINI CRUMBLES

Quintessentially English, fruit crumbles are a rustic, homely pudding generally served in a steaming mound with lashings of custard. Here we've refined the traditional recipe, mixing the fruit with sweet white wine and chocolate for a touch of luxury and breaking up a crisp baked crumble mixture into shards. Every bit as tasty as the original, but with just enough finesse to grace a royal table.

Serves 4

For the crumble

40g unsalted butter, cubed

40g golden caster sugar

40g plain flour

25g oats

a pinch of cinnamon

15g light soft brown sugar

20g hazelnuts, finely chopped

For the fruit and chocolate layer

15g unsalted butter

15g light soft brown sugar

2 eating apples, such as Cox, chopped

200g blackberries

2 tbsp sweet white wine

25g white chocolate, finely chopped, plus extra to sprinkle

To serve

75ml double cream

½ tsp icing sugar

Preheat the oven to 200°C/fan 180°C/gas 6. Line a baking sheet with baking parchment.

Put the butter, caster sugar and flour into a bowl and rub everything together with your hands until the butter is roughly incorporated into the mixture. Stir in the oats, cinnamon, light soft brown sugar and hazelnuts and roughly rub it all together again to combine.

Spread the crumble out on the parchment into an even half-centimetre layer and bake in the oven for 10–15 minutes until golden. Slide the parchment on to a wire rack to cool, then tip the crumble into a bowl and use a spoon to break it up into pieces to make a rough crumble, leaving four pieces whole for decoration.

For the fruit and chocolate layer, melt the butter and sugar together in a pan over a low heat and stir in the chopped apples. Cook for 2–3 minutes until the apples have turned golden and started to caramelise. Stir in the blackberries and wine and turn up the heat slightly. Add the chocolate, allow to melt and stir to make a sauce.

To serve, whip the double cream and icing sugar together in a bowl until moussey and thick. Divide the fruit and chocolate mixture between four dessert glasses. Sprinkle over the crumble, reserving the four large pieces. Put a spoonful of the whipped cream on top of the crumble, then slide a large piece of crumble on to it. Sprinkle more white chocolate over the top before serving.

CHOCOLATE AND CHERRY FRANGIPANE TARTLETS

After her death, Queen Anne's confectioner, Mary Eales, published a book of the sweet recipes she'd prepared for the sugar-loving monarch. Among them are several almond concoctions and here combines the queen's favourite almond paste with chocolate and a fruity conserve. Crowned with fresh cherries, these dainty tartlets are fit for a queen.

———————————— ♔ ————————————

Makes 12

For the pastry

125g plain flour

a pinch of salt

50g chilled unsalted butter, cut into cubes

1 medium egg yolk, at room temperature

For the frangipane filling and decoration

40g unsalted butter, at room temperature

40g golden caster sugar

1 medium egg, at room temperature, beaten

40g plain flour

15g cocoa powder

20g ground almonds

1 tsp baking powder

about 4 tbsp good-quality cherry conserve

20g white chocolate

12 fresh cherries

Whizz the flour, salt and butter in a food processor until the mixture resembles breadcrumbs. Whisk the egg yolk with 1 teaspoon of cold water, then add to the food processor and whizz again to mix in with the other ingredients.

Tip the mixture into a bowl and bring it together with your hands, kneading gently to make a smooth dough. Shape into a flat disc, then wrap in parchment and chill in the fridge for 20 minutes.

Unwrap the pastry and roll it out thinly until it measures 2–3mm. Cut out twelve 7cm rounds and push into each hole of a 12-hole bun tin.

Put the tin in the fridge to chill for up to 30 minutes. Preheat the oven to 180°C/fan 160°C/gas 4.

To make the frangipane filling, beat the butter and sugar together in a bowl until soft and creamy. Gradually beat in the egg, adding a little flour if the mixture looks like it is going to curdle, then add the remaining flour, along with the cocoa powder, ground almonds and baking powder. Beat well until the mixture is smooth.

Take the lined tin out of the fridge and spoon about half a teaspoon of conserve into each pastry case. Put about 1 heaped teaspoonful of filling on top of the conserve in each pastry case, smoothing down gently. Transfer to the oven and bake for 20 minutes.

Allow the tartlets to cool in the tin, then melt the white chocolate in the microwave on the lowest setting. Spoon a little chocolate over each tartlet, then push a cherry on top of it. Leave to set then serve.

THE CHOCOLATE MAKERS

Making chocolate required a great deal of culinary flair: the people who handled it had to be skilled and knowledgeable. The best chocolate makers were able to source the finest cacao beans and devise the best recipes for making chocolate to drink. William III's chocolate maker was given an expensive bed, a luxury only given to the most important servants.

The beans themselves needed lengthy and complex preparation before they could be made into a drink. The chocolate maker, probably with some assistance, roasted the beans slowly and gently in a bean roaster over a spit. In the most expensive recipes, the beans were coated with aromatic oils and essences before roasting. Once roasted, the husks were removed to reveal the nut-like nibs. The nibs were then ground over heat, either in a pestle and mortar or, following the Mesoamerican method, using a metate – a stone slab and roller. This was a process that took hours to produce a smooth paste – the longer the grinding the smoother and better the chocolate. The paste was then flavoured. King Charles II favoured vanilla, ambergris (from the intestinal tract of a sperm whale) and civet (a secretion from the glands of a type of African cat). Both these rare and exotic items gave the chocolate a musky aroma. Sugar was added and the paste was formed into discs, known as cakes, and then left for a month for the flavours to mature.

Until the nineteenth century, the cakes would usually be melted in water, wine or milk and made into a chocolate drink, usually thickened with egg yolk. Though this drink was rich and luscious, the 'cakes' were sometimes used instead to flavour meringues or to make a custard called chocolate cream. 'Chocolate cream' features in the bills of fare (daily royal menus) for Kensington Palace in the 1730s: chocolate was grated over sweetened custard and served from elegant glasses to George II and his courtiers.

After preparation chocolate had a tendency to separate and needed frequent whisking. This meant the chocolate maker often needed to be on hand to whisk the chocolate, giving him close personal contact with the monarch and direct access to the most private rooms in the palace. The importance of the chocolate maker was further demonstrated by the ranking of the role within the service hierarchy. The position fell under the stewardship of the Lord Chamberlain rather than the Lord Steward. The latter was responsible for most culinary professionals, such as the cook, while the Lord Chamberlain was responsible for ceremonial positions and the monarch's personal servants. This administrative quirk reflects the fact that chocolate at court was much more than just food; it was a luxury for sophisticated tastes, prepared with the utmost care.

Chocolate remained relatively expensive until the nineteenth century when it became mass produced by chocolate factories, such as Cadbury. Until then, great quantities of cacao beans were required to make comparatively small amounts of chocolate. In 1689, a merchants' petition against increased duties on tea, coffee and chocolate stated that while a pound of coffee made two and a half gallons of the beverage and a pound of tea made nine gallons, a pound of chocolate only made one gallon.

At the royal court, the equipment used to serve the chocolate was suitably luxurious. The king and queen often drank it in the morning, either in private or with especially chosen company. To be asked to drink chocolate with the king was a sign of your importance. It was sometimes drunk alongside tea and coffee as an accompaniment to courtly entertainments, such as card playing which would take place in the glamorous settings of the state apartments of the palaces. Although probably made in copper pots, chocolate was served from silver, or silver gilt chocolate pots, made by the finest and most fashionable craftsmen. Late seventeenth and early eighteenth century chocolate pots are distinguished from tea and coffee pots by having an extra, small, hinged lid at the top of the pot. This allowed for the insertion of a stirrer, sometimes known as a molinet, which enabled the chocolate maker to whisk the chocolate just before serving. The foaming chocolate would then be poured into small porcelain cups.

The 1721 Jewel House inventory of plate across all palaces mentions 'six chocolate frames', or cup holders, used for cradling porcelain cups (which at this date rarely had handles) filled with chocolate. The fine and brightly decorated cups themselves would likely to have either been an import from China or, up until the 1740s, from Dresden, given as a diplomatic gift.

The precious objects point to the value of the chocolate drink and the status of the people to whom it was served. Whisking the chocolate in the pot and balancing porcelain in a cradle all require a certain amount of dexterity to avoid spills, suggesting that there was a particular elegance and etiquette to chocolate drinking. A courtier would be expected to drink his chocolate daintily without spills. The expensive and beautiful equipment from which chocolate was served was fitting to the settings in which chocolate was drunk at court, either in the exclusive company of the king or as part of a lavish courtly event.

PUFF PASTRY PEAR TARTS

Poaching pears in red wine turns them a striking deep purple colour and gives them something of a 'wow' factor. They make a stylish topping for these elegant tarts, which despite their sophisticated appearance are delightfully simple to prepare.

Serves 4

For the poached pears

2 small pears

125ml red wine

50g sugar

1 cinnamon stick

For the tarts

25g unsalted butter

25g sugar

1 tbsp beaten egg, at room temperature

20g ground almonds

15g plain flour

10g white chocolate, finely chopped

½ x 320g ready-rolled all-butter puff pastry

Peel and halve the pears then cut out the core, but take care not to remove the stalks. Put in a pan and add the red wine, 100ml of water, the sugar and cinnamon stick. Cover with a piece of baking parchment and simmer for 15–20 minutes until the pears are tender. Leave to cool in the liquor.

Beat the butter, sugar and egg together. Stir in the ground almonds, plain flour and white chocolate.

Preheat the oven to 210°C/fan 190°C/gas 7. Preheat a baking sheet.

Unroll the puff pastry on a board and stamp out four 9cm rounds using a scone cutter. Spread the almond mixture over the middle of each round, leaving a 1cm border. Lift the pears out of the liquor and slice on a board several times from the stalk down to the base, without cutting through completely at the top. Put one pear on top of each round, cut side down, pressing down on the slices so they fan out.

Slide the tarts on to the preheated baking sheet and bake for around 20 minutes until they are golden and puffed up.

Meanwhile, bring the poaching liquor to the boil and simmer for 2–3 minutes until syrupy. Brush a little of the glaze over the tarts, then serve the remainder drizzled over the top.

TEATIME BITES
AND
BISCUITS

CHOCOLATE AND COFFEE BOURBONS

Over 100 years old, the sandwich-style Bourbon is a much-loved national icon. Created in 1910 by the London confectionery company Peek Frean, it was initially called the Creola, until it was changed to the name of the French royal family. Peek Frean furthered its royal connections by making Queen Elizabeth II's wedding cake in 1947. We've added coffee to reduce the sweetness, but you can leave it out if you want to stay true to tradition.

Makes 8–10

60g unsalted butter

1 tbsp golden syrup

1 tbsp boiling water

100g plain flour, plus extra to sprinkle

30g cocoa powder

½ tsp instant espresso coffee

¼ tsp bicarbonate of soda

40g golden caster sugar

For the filling

25g unsalted butter, at room temperature

75g icing sugar

1 tbsp cocoa powder

a good pinch of coffee powder

a pinch of salt

1 tbsp hot water

about 1 tbsp milk

Put the butter in a pan with the golden syrup and 1 tablespoon of boiling water and heat gently to melt the butter. Set aside to cool.

Put the flour, cocoa, coffee, bicarbonate of soda and sugar in a food processor and whizz to combine.

Pour in the butter mixture and whizz again until the mixture comes together into a ball of dough. Shape the dough into a rough disc, wrap in baking parchment and chill for 30 minutes.

Line two baking sheets with baking parchment. Remove the dough from the baking parchment, sprinkle the paper with a little flour, replace the dough and sprinkle with a little more flour. Cover with another sheet of baking parchment and roll the dough to 2mm thick. If the dough feels very dry and starts to crack, wet your hands and knead again to moisten it.

Use a ruler to cut 16–20 rectangles measuring 6.5 x 3cm, rerolling the dough as necessary. Use a skewer to push holes down the edge of each rectangle for decoration. Chill on the baking sheets for 15 minutes.

Preheat the oven to 190°C/fan 170°C/gas 5. Bake the biscuits for 10–12 minutes, then cool on a wire rack.

For the filling, beat the butter in a bowl to soften, then gradually beat in the icing sugar, then the cocoa powder. Dissolve the coffee and salt in the hot water and beat into the butter with the milk. Spoon the filling into a piping bag fitted with a 3mm nozzle and pipe around the edge of half the biscuits, with a squeeze in the middle. Top with uniced biscuits. Leave to set.

CHOCOLATE AND PISTACHIO SHORTBREAD

The key to ensuring shortbread keeps its beautiful pale golden colour is to bake it very slowly so that the heat just combines and sets the ingredients, rather than colours or toasts them as it does in other biscuits.

Makes 16

175g unsalted butter, softened, plus extra to grease

75g golden caster sugar, plus extra to dust

200g plain flour

50g cornflour

To decorate

200g dark chocolate (minimum 70 per cent cocoa solids)

75–100g salted pistachio nuts, skinned and chopped

Preheat the oven to 150°C/fan 130°C/gas 2. Lightly grease a square 18cm tin.

Put the butter into a bowl and beat in the sugar using a wooden spoon. Sift over the flour and cornflour and slowly work into the butter mixture until you make a smooth paste. Bring it together with your hands if it looks a little crumbly at the end.

Spoon the mixture into the greased tin, pressing it into the edges evenly with the back of a spoon, then mark into 16 squares with a table knife.

Prick each square about three times with a fork, then put in the oven to bake for 1 hour. After 30 minutes, mark the squares again, go over the same pricks with a fork then return to the oven to finish baking.

Lift out of the tin and transfer to a wire rack. Allow to cool, then put on a board and carefully chop into 16 squares.

Melt the chocolate in a heatproof bowl set over a pan of simmering water, making sure the base of the bowl doesn't touch the water. Take the bowl off the pan and cool for 5 minutes.

To decorate, dip each shortbread square diagonally into the chocolate then sprinkle with pistachio nuts. Allow to set on a tray lined with baking parchment before serving.

CHOCOLATE AND WALNUT COOKIES

Ground almonds replace flour in this recipe, which makes these nutty little biscuits light as a feather. They're wonderfully easy to prepare and are perfect for a quick teatime treat or a little pick-me-up with a mid-morning coffee.

Makes 14

125g icing sugar

2 tbsp cocoa powder

2 tbsp ground almonds

a pinch of ground ginger

a good pinch of salt

40g walnut halves, plus extra to decorate

1 large egg white lightly whisked, at room temperature

Preheat the oven to 170°C/fan 150°C/gas 3. Line a large baking sheet with baking parchment.

Sift the icing sugar and cocoa powder into a large bowl. Do the same with the ground almonds, ginger and salt. Finely chop 40g of walnuts and stir in.

Make a well in the middle and pour in the egg white. Mix with a wooden spoon until all the icing sugar has dissolved and the mixture looks like a lumpy batter. Scoop up a generous heaped half teaspoon of the mixture and spoon on top of the parchment. Press a walnut half on top. Continue until all the mixture is used up and all the cookies are topped with walnuts.

Bake for 8 minutes. Leave to cool on the tray then arrange on a plate and serve.

ORANGE BISCUITS WITH CHOCOLATE CHIPS

Dark chocolate is paired with its tried and trusted partner, orange, to make a lovely rounded little biscuit that's perfect at any time of the day. It's important to plump for a dark chocolate with a high cocoa percentage, though, to make sure the biscuits aren't too sweet.

Makes around 25-30

125g unsalted butter, softened

50g golden granulated sugar

50g soft light brown sugar

1 medium egg, beaten

½ tsp vanilla extract

a good pinch of salt

175g plain flour

grated zest of 1 orange

75g dark chocolate (70 per cent cocoa solids), roughly chopped, or use chocolate chips

Preheat the oven to 190°C/fan 170°C/gas 5. Line two baking sheets with baking parchment.

Put the butter and the sugars into a large bowl and cream together using an electric hand whisk. Quickly whisk in the egg, vanilla extract and salt, scraping down the sides of the bowl.

Add the flour, orange zest and chocolate and fold together using a wooden spoon to make a soft dough.

Take teaspoonfuls of the mixture and roll them into rounds. Place on the baking sheet and flatten slightly. Bake in the oven for around 15 minutes, until just golden round the edges. Store in an airtight tin for up to five days.

WHITE CHOCOLATE SCONES WITH STRAWBERRIES AND CLOTTED CREAM

Devonshire and Cornish tearooms may recoil in horror at the thought of straying from the quintessential fruit or plain scone recipe, but we think that adding a little white chocolate to the original is a lovely way to ring the changes. Don't stray too far from tearoom tradition, however; scones simply aren't scones without the accompanying clotted cream, jam and pot of tea.

Makes 8-10

250g self-raising flour

50g unsalted butter

2 tbsp golden caster sugar

50g white chocolate, chopped

around 175ml milk, plus extra to brush

1 tsp vanilla extract

To serve

clotted cream

strawberry jam

fresh strawberries

Preheat the oven to 220°C/fan 200°C/gas 7. Line a baking sheet with baking parchment.

Sift the flour into a bowl and rub in the butter. Stir in the sugar and chocolate.

Make a well in the centre and pour in the milk and vanilla extract. Mix quickly with a knife until the mixture comes together then knead very briefly. Turn the lump of dough out on to a board and shape into a round, about 2.5cm thick.

Dip a 6cm cutter into the flour then use it to stamp out 8-10 rounds. Put them on the baking sheet, brush with milk and bake for 12-15 minutes until risen and just golden.

Serve just warm with the clotted cream, jam and fresh strawberries.

CHOCOLATE HOUSES

Before the 1600s, a man living in a major English city who wanted to socialise would head for the alehouse. However, the arrival of a new, non-alcoholic drink – coffee – in around 1620 changed the male social scene. Drinkers of this bitter beverage, initially imported from Turkey, enjoyed the feeling of being pepped up without the debilitating hangovers the next day.

Picture previous page: The Chocolate Kitchen, Hampton Court Palace

Coffee fuelled discussion and by 1652 convivial 'coffee houses' were on every city corner, also selling the other 'exotic' beverages - tea and more rarely chocolate. In general, these were egalitarian environments where discussion of the latest news, scientific endeavour or political intrigue was rife, much to the consternation of the monarchy. Charles II tried without success to suppress coffee houses.

By the end of the 1690s, specific houses opened in London near St James's Palace that were purveyors of pleasure, as well as chocolate. By comparison to the raucous coffee houses, they were smartly decorated and attracted an elite, aristocratic clientele. Some, such as Ozindas, became places where artworks were sold. The most famous of these houses, Whites, opened in 1692 and it exists today as an elite gentleman's club. Jonathan Swift referred to Whites as 'the bane of half the nobility' because of its reputation for gambling and for the 'beautiful, neat, well-dressed and amiable, but very dangerous nymphs', who could be purchased alongside your cup of chocolate.

In some ways the chocolate houses mirrored the ways in which chocolate was drunk at court. At Kensington Palace, for example, the Earl of Clarendon reported that 'Dice, cards and danse, were the divertisements; Tea Chacolate & other liquors, and sweetmeats were the entertainments and refreshments.'

One particular chocolate house in Greenwich consciously tried to mimic the court, exploiting royal connections. It was owned by Thomas Tosier, who was appointed chocolate maker to George I in 1717. While he was away whisking up chocolate at court, his feisty wife Grace ran the business in Greenwich.

Commercially astute, Grace styled herself 'Wife of the King's Chocolate Maker', even after Thomas died, and on her remarriage she kept the name Tosier. As well as serving chocolate, she hosted balls in her chocolate house, to coincide with events such as the king's birthday. By offering this 'courtly' experience, Grace was able to attract an impressive clientele including Prince Frederick, son of George II, as well as many other English noblemen and women and foreign dignitaries who also attended court.

Grace became a celebrity in her own right. She was famous for her 'large-brimmed hat' and for having 'flowers in her bosom'. She had at least two portraits painted of her by the society artist Bartholomew Dandridge, and one of these was made into a print and circulated as part of a series of portraits of famous Londoners.

CHOCOLATE, RUM AND ALMOND TRUFFLES

Lady Ann Fanshawe, wife of the Spanish ambassador during the late 1600s, recounted how nobles in the Spanish court were often given chocolate as a *'regalo'* or regal gift to demonstrate the giver's generosity. The chocolate in those days needed a lot of work to transform it into an edible confection or drink, but there's nothing time-consuming about these tasty truffles. Parcelled up in cellophane bags with ribbons, the white-chocolate-dipped balls would make a very generous and attractive gift of your own.

Makes 12

20g raisins, chopped

1 tsp rum

1–2 tbsp beaten egg, at room temperature

70–80g ground almonds

30g golden caster sugar

10g golden icing sugar

125g good-quality white chocolate

Put the raisins in a medium bowl and stir in the rum. Leave to marinate for at least one hour, or overnight if possible.

Add 1 tablespoon of the egg to the bowl with the raisins, along with 70g of the ground almonds and the sugars, and beat well. The mixture should feel firm and a little sticky. Add more beaten egg if you think it needs it or, if it's very sticky, add the extra 10g of ground almonds.

Divide the mixture into roughly 12 pieces and roll each one into a ball. Put on a plate and freeze for 1–2 hours until the mixture has firmed up.

Break up the white chocolate and put in a bowl. Heat on the lowest setting in the microwave until almost all of the chocolate has melted. Stir in the remaining bits until smooth.

Drop each almond ball into the chocolate and toss to coat, then put on a board lined with baking parchment. Drizzle over a little white chocolate to decorate.

Allow the chocolate to set completely then serve.

CHOCOLATE AND CARDAMOM CHELSEA BUNS

Plump, sugary buns have been enjoyed in England since the fifteenth century and many, such as the Chelsea and Bath buns, are named after the place they were first made. Kings George II and III and their families are thought to have visited London's Chelsea Bun House, to snack on a sticky, fruity sweet bread. Here we've replaced the sugary glaze with chocolate and added cardamom for an aromatic twist.

Makes 8

25g unsalted butter, plus extra to grease

1 tsp active dried yeast

25g golden caster sugar

175–200ml lukewarm milk

250g strong white bread flour, plus extra for dusting

½ tsp salt

For the filling

6 dried figs

juice of 1 orange

1 tbsp brandy

the seeds from 3 cardamom pods, ground with a pinch of salt

50g milk chocolate

10g unsalted butter, melted

demerara sugar, to sprinkle

Grease a round 20cm cake tin and line the base with baking parchment.

Put the yeast into a small bowl with 1 teaspoon of the sugar. Stir in 50ml of the warm milk. Set aside for the yeast to activate. Stir the butter into the remaining milk.

Sift the flour into a bowl. Stir in the salt and remaining sugar. Make a well in the centre and pour in the yeast mixture, followed by the milk. Mix together with your hands then knead on a board or use a freestanding mixer with a dough hook until the dough feels smooth. Add a light dusting of flour if it is too sticky to knead. Put in a clean bowl, cover and allow to rise for 40 minutes.

Meanwhile, prepare the filling. Put the figs in a pan with the orange juice, brandy and cardamom. Place over a medium heat and bring to the boil. Turn off the heat, then cool. Whizz in a blender to finely chop the figs, then add the chocolate and whizz again to combine.

Roll out the dough on a lightly floured board to measure 30 x 21cm. Spread the fig mixture all over the dough then roll it up from the bottom. Cut into 8 rounds and arrange them cut-side up in the tin. Cover and leave to prove for 30 minutes.

Preheat the oven to 200°C/fan 180°C/gas 6 and bake the buns for 30 minutes. Brush the cooked buns with melted butter and sprinkle with sugar. Remove from the tin and cool on a wire rack for 5 minutes before serving.

ICED CROWN BISCUITS

Depending on how proficient you are at piping, you might need a little practice before the white outline on these crunchy little biscuits looks perfectly neat and tidy, but once you get the hang of it, you will be impressing friends and family with all kinds of iced creations. These biscuits can be stored in an airtight tin for up to four days, and using different-shaped cutters would make lovely gifts for any occasion.

Makes 26–30

40g unsalted butter, at room temperature, plus extra to grease

50g caster sugar

10g white chocolate, finely grated

a pinch of salt

½ tsp vanilla extract

1–1½ tbsp beaten egg yolk, at room temperature

75g plain flour, plus extra for dusting

To decorate

1 medium egg white, at room temperature

200g white icing sugar

a selection of edible colours

Beat the butter, sugar and white chocolate together in a bowl until the mixture looks soft and creamy. Stir in the salt, vanilla extract and beaten egg yolk. Sift over the flour and stir in. Keep stirring until the mixture turns crumbly and starts to form a dough. Bring together with your hands and knead until smooth. Shape into a flat disc, then wrap in cling film and chill for 20 minutes.

Preheat the oven to 180°C/fan 160°C/gas 6. Lightly grease a baking sheet.

Roll out the dough on a lightly floured board until it's 2–3mm thick. Stamp out the biscuits using a 4cm crown cutter (measuring from the middle point down to the base). Transfer to the baking sheet and bake for 8–10 minutes until just golden around the edges. Cool on a wire rack – they'll firm up once they've cooled.

To decorate, put the egg white into a large bowl and gradually whisk in the icing sugar using an electric whisk. Continue to whisk in the icing sugar until the mixture is very thick.

Put about a sixth of the icing into a piping bag fitted with a 2mm nozzle and pipe three dots on to the points of each biscuit, then draw an outline round the edge. Divide the remaining icing among four or five bowls and add a dash of colour to each with a skewer or cocktail stick. Mix to your desired hue, then add a tiny splash of water to loosen the icing. Spoon each colour into the outline of four or five biscuits, teasing it out to fill the space. Leave to set before enjoying.

CHOCOLATE AND ALMOND MERINGUES

There is some debate over the origin of the meringue. While the French, Swiss and the Polish all claim credit for being the first to whisk together egg whites and sugar, the earliest documented recipe appeared in England in 1604. What we do know is that royalty across Europe have delighted in this sugary delicacy for centuries. King George II and his courtiers were enjoying chocolate-flavoured meringues during the eighteenth century, while Queen Marie Antoinette is said to have made her own at her Trianon estate at Versailles. These elegant miniature meringue sandwiches would surely have satisfied monarchs on both sides of the Channel.

Makes around 40

15g chopped whole almonds

2 medium egg whites, at room temperature

100g golden caster sugar

1 tsp cocoa powder

For the filling

20–30g dark chocolate (minimum 60 per cent cocoa solids)

Preheat the oven to 110°C/fan 90°C/gas ½. Line a flat baking sheet with baking parchment.

Pulse the chopped almonds in a blender until finely chopped, taking care not to overwhizz otherwise the nuts will end up oily.

Whisk the egg whites in a clean grease-free bowl, just until the mixture stands in soft peaks. Add the sugar, a tablespoon at a time, and whisk in until dissolved.

Sift the cocoa powder over the top then add most of the chopped almonds, leaving about a teaspoon to sprinkle over at the end.

Fold everything together then spoon into a piping bag fitted with a 1cm nozzle.

Pipe rounds on to the parchment, sprinkle with the remaining nuts then bake in the oven for around 1 hour. They're ready when the meringues come away easily from the parchment. Leave in the oven to cool.

Melt the chocolate gently on the lowest setting in the microwave. Carefully spread a little chocolate on the base of one meringue, then put another meringue on top. Put aside to set. Continue until you've filled all the meringues, then serve.

CHOCOLATE,
THE WONDER DRUG

When chocolate was introduced into England some early
commentators praised its medicinal properties, even
pronouncing it a wonder drug. Royal physician Henry
Strubbe, writing to the Royal Society in 1668, claimed, 'If
it [chocolate] were well made and taken in a right way,
it is the best diet for hyppchondriacs [sic] and chronical
disptempers [sic], and the scurvy, gout and stone, and
women lying in.' Chocolate was prescribed for good
health well into the mid-eighteenth century. However, as
well as being a luxury drink it was also a luxury medicine,
and only the wealthy could afford it.

The earliest evidence available suggesting that chocolate was prescribed at court is from a list of silver equipment supplied to the apothecary James Chase in 1687, during the reign of King James II (r1685–1688). The order included a 'glyster pot', 'infusion pot' and '1 chocolate pot both white and guilt'. Other orders included medical items such as syringes, a 'pessell and mortar' and an 'eye cupp'. The role of the court apothecary was to prepare the medicines prescribed by the court physicians, and James Chase also prepared special spices for the king and probably prepared the chocolate that was prescribed by the royal physicians.

Sir Hans Sloane, physician to King George I, was particularly interested in chocolate. He seems to have had his own special recipe that was much appreciated. Among Sloane's papers are thank-you letters from Johann Georg Steigerthal, George I's personal doctor in Hanover, for presents of 'your chocolate' accompanied by bottles of Madeira wine

However, some royal doctors were not convinced by the health claims. Govard Bidloo, personal physician to William III, felt that the king drank too much sweet chocolate and needed more exercise, although the chocoholic king ignored his protests: 'Finding HM [His Majesty] well, I recommended him to go for a horse ride, which he did around 11am ... before he left having drunk some chocolate ... In the evening HM told me: "I'm gaining back my old way of life" and HM's legs were very un-swollen, despite this he still had chocolate again around 7pm, even though I advised against it.'

Some contemporary writers were entirely suspicious of chocolate, blaming it or linking it to the deaths of monarchs. The political writer Roger Coke said disparagingly of Queen Anne: 'Her life would have lasted longer, if she had not eaten so much ... She supped too much chocolate, and died monstrously fat.'

George II's death was particularly undignified, if socialite and historian Horace Walpole is to be believed: 'On the 25th of October he rose as usual at six, and drank his chocolate; for all his actions were invariably methodic.' Then hearing 'a noise louder than the Royal Wind' his German valet ran into the king's water closet and found him lying dead on the floor.

These scathing comments, linking chocolate to ill health and even death, emphasise that it was still considered a foreign import, and to the eighteenth-century mind, likely to be dangerous, despite the huge enjoyment of chocolate at court, and among the aristocracy. Even today we still regard chocolate as a little decadent, or certainly only to be enjoyed in moderation.

CRANBERRY AND CHOCOLATE FLAPJACKS

Chewy, sticky and moist, these buttery oaty bars are one of the most versatile and easiest bakes you can make. Change the fruit, seeds and chocolate according to your preference and adjust the cooking time so that they are as firm or as sticky as you desire.

***

Makes 28

235g unsalted butter, plus extra to grease

150g porridge oats

200g jumbo oats

grated zest of 1 orange

1 tsp ground mixed spice

50g dried cranberries, roughly chopped

2 tbsp pumpkin seeds

2 tbsp sunflower seeds

2 tbsp linseeds

200g demerara sugar

50g set honey

50g dark chocolate chips (minimum 70 per cent cocoa solids)

Preheat the oven to 190°C/fan 170°C/gas 5. Lightly grease a 20 x 30cm baking tin and line with baking parchment.

Put the oats, orange zest, mixed spice and cranberries into a bowl. Stir in the pumpkin seeds, sunflower seeds and linseeds.

Melt the butter in a pan with the demerara sugar and honey over a low heat. As soon as the butter has melted, stir everything together and pour into the bowl with the oat mixture. Stir well, then add the chocolate chips and stir again.

Spoon the mixture into the prepared tin, spreading it out into the corners so it's level, and bake in the oven for 20–25 minutes until golden. Mark into 28 squares and leave to cool. As the mixture cools it will set firm.

Transfer to a wooden board and cut into squares with a sharp knife.

CHOCOLATE MENDIANTS

These little discs of melted chocolate are traditionally made as part of the Provence region's '13 desserts' – a Christmas custom in which they are topped with four specific dried fruits and nuts representing the different colours of the robes worn by four mendicant monastic orders. Although 'mendiant' means beggar in French, a crystallised rose petal and a sprinkling of edible gold dust give our recipe a truly majestic finish.

———————————— ♔ ————————————

Makes 10

50g dark chocolate (minimum 60 per cent cocoa solids)

10g good-quality white chocolate

crystallised rose petals

edible gold dust

Line a board or baking sheet with baking parchment and draw ten 4cm circles, spaced apart, on to it. Turn the parchment over so the drawing is on the other side.

Break up the dark chocolate and put into a bowl. Place in the microwave and melt on the lowest heat setting for about 3–4 minutes, checking it often to make sure the chocolate doesn't overheat, until almost all of it has melted. Stir in the unmelted bits until smooth.

Put the white chocolate in a bowl and melt it in the microwave for 10-20 seconds.

Take a teaspoon and quickly spoon a thin layer of the dark chocolate into the outlined circles, smoothing it out to the edges.

Put a small drop of white chocolate in the middle and use a skewer to tease lines out towards the edge. Put a piece of rose petal in the middle and leave to set.

Very gently lift each mendiant off the parchment and arrange on a plate. Sprinkle with the edible gold dust and serve.

SALTED CARAMEL BROWNIES

The world's love of the irresistible combination of flaky sea salt and creamy, buttery caramel is showing no sign of waning. From the United States to Japan, via Europe, salted caramel pops up in every sweet guise you can imagine: ice creams, milkshakes, chocolates and as a decadent sauce. Here it finds its most seductive outlet in brownies – velvety and rich, chewy yet with a crisp crust, these treats are sinfully moreish.

Makes 20

For the salted caramel

1 tbsp light soft brown sugar

2 tbsp dark muscovado sugar

100ml double cream

2 large pinches of sea salt

For the brownies

175g unsalted butter, chopped, plus extra to grease

275g dark chocolate (minimum 60 per cent cocoa solids), finely chopped

225g golden caster sugar

3 medium eggs, at room temperature

175g plain flour

25g cocoa powder

Preheat the oven to 180°C/fan 160°C/gas 4. Grease and line a 21cm square baking tin with baking parchment.

To make the salted caramel, put the sugars in a small frying pan with 1 teaspoon of water. Put over a low heat and watch carefully until the sugar has melted and starts to bubble. Stir in the cream and salt and bring to the boil, then simmer for 2–3 minutes until the mixture has thickened and looks saucy.

For the brownies, put the butter in a pan with the chocolate and melt very gently. Set aside to cool a little.

Whisk the sugar and eggs in a large bowl using an electric hand whisk until the mixture is thick, moussey and leaves a ribbon-like trail when the whisk is lifted.

Sift the flour and cocoa powder into the bowl, then pour the chocolate mixture in. Fold everything together making sure that all the flour has been mixed in.

Spoon the mixture into the prepared tin then tap the base to ensure it sits evenly. Put spoonfuls of the caramel all over the top then, using a skewer, marble it through the brownie mixture.

Bake in the oven for 25 minutes. Cool in the tin, then transfer to a board and cut into 20 portions.

DRINKS
AND
SAUCES

CREAM OF CHOCOLATE LIQUEUR

A home-made liqueur is a delightfully celebratory way to round off a meal, either on its own or accompanied by a dainty petit four, such as a Chocolate Mendiant (see page 90) or a Chocolate and Almond Meringue (see page 84).

Makes around 375ml

2 tbsp cocoa powder

1 tbsp demerara sugar

100ml condensed milk

75ml double cream

4 tbsp brandy

40g dark chocolate (minimum 70 per cent cocoa solids), finely chopped

Sterilise a 400ml bottle and set aside. Chill four small glasses.

Put the cocoa powder, demerara sugar, condensed milk and cream in a pan. Bring to the boil, whisking all the time to mix everything together until smooth.

Slowly stir in the brandy and dark chocolate and allow the heat of the pan to melt the chocolate. Pour in 125ml of water and simmer, whisking well, for 2–3 minutes until the liqueur thickens slightly.

Stir again, then pour the mixture into the sterilised bottle. Seal and allow to cool.

Divide the liqueur evenly among the chilled glasses and serve. The liqueur will last, unopened, for up to four days in the fridge

A NEW CENTURY
OF CHOCOLATE

The increased industrialisation across England in the nineteenth century, particularly the development of hydraulic steam power, hastened and improved the processing of chocolate. Quaker Joseph Fry was the first of the English chocolate makers to exploit the new technology. In 1789, he purchased a Watt's steam engine to grind cacao beans. The fine powder he produced was mixed with cacao butter, producing a thin, less viscous substance that, significantly, could be cast into moulds, and by 1849 his grandsons Francis and Joseph had made the world's first chocolate bar, which carried the extravagant name 'Chocolat Délicieux à Manger'.

In 1828, the Dutch chemists Casparus and Coenraad Johannes van Houten invented a hydraulic press for removing cocoa fat from ground chocolate. This made the chocolate liquor less oily and less prone to separation when mixed with liquids. Previously the fat could only be removed by the arduous process of boiling and skimming, which is why the earliest drinking chocolate required constant whisking to stop it from separating.

The Birmingham-based Quaker firm of Cadbury adopted the van Houten method and created a powdered chocolate drink called 'Cadbury's chocolate essence'. They, too, created their own moulded chocolate and in 1868 Richard Cadbury began to sell boxes of chocolate, decorated with a picture of his daughter holding a kitten!

Much of the success of the Quaker companies can be attributed to their beliefs. Eschewing alcohol, they were initially interested in promoting chocolate as a cheaper, wholesome alternative to gin, the scourge of the working classes. This desire to improve lives motivated their drive to exploit new technology, the better to produce inexpensive chocolate.

A strong sense of duty and ethics ran throughout Quaker firms; for example, they refused to buy cocoa from plantations that used slaves and Rowntree and Cadbury used their profits to ensure good conditions for their workers. They also provided housing and facilities for staff by creating the 'model' villages of Bourneville and New Earswick.

Cadbury's prestige was confirmed when Queen Victoria (r1837–1901) appointed them royal purveyors of chocolate in 1853. Queen Victoria loved cake – and chocolate cake was a definite favourite. As a princess, Victoria endured a strict, highly-disciplined upbringing, with her every move controlled by the adults around her. However, when she became queen she made up for lost time! For one tea party (for an unknown number of guests) at Buckingham Palace she ordered, '16 chocolate sponges, 12 plain sponges, 16 fondant biscuits, one box of wafers … one and a half dozen flat finger biscuits … one princess cake and one rice'.

CHOCOLATE MILKSHAKE

Using both milk and dark chocolate blended with a rich chocolate syrup and ice cream makes this a deliciously decadent drink. Milkshakes need to be served frothy and ice cold, so have your glasses and guests at the ready when you pour this cooling summery sweet treat.

Serves 4

For the chocolate syrup

75g golden caster sugar

2 tbsp cocoa powder

For the milkshake

800ml milk

75g dark chocolate (minimum 60 per cent cocoa solids), finely chopped, plus extra to serve

2 balls of vanilla ice cream, plus extra to serve

Sterilise a 300ml jar and set aside. Chill four large glasses.

To make the syrup, put the sugar into a pan with 150ml of water. Heat gently to dissolve the sugar then bring to the boil and simmer for 3–5 minutes until syrupy. Stir in the cocoa powder then simmer again for a further minute. Pour into a sterilised jar and allow to cool.

To make the milkshake, put the milk, dark chocolate and ice cream into a blender. Add 6 tablespoons of the chocolate syrup and blend until smooth.

Divide the milkshake among the four chilled glasses and top with more ice cream and grated chocolate before serving.

CHOCOLATE ESPRESSO MARTINI

Though a very distant relation of the drink that 007 shook over ice, this caffeine hit in a cocktail is very striking when served in a traditional Martini glass. To make a homemade chocolate liqueur, add 3–4 tablespoons of vodka to the chocolate syrup recipe on page 101.

Serves 2

8 whole espresso beans

15g dark chocolate (minimum 70 per cent cocoa solids), grated

4–6 ice cubes

15ml chocolate liqueur, such as crème de cacao (or see recipe introduction)

50ml espresso

25ml vodka

Put the espresso beans in a pan and heat gently for 1–2 minutes to toast.

Put half the beans into a cocktail shaker, followed by the dark chocolate, ice cubes, chocolate liqueur, espresso and vodka.

Put the lid on the shaker and shake well for a couple of minutes. Strain between two Martini glasses and serve topped with the remaining beans.

Picture previous page: The Orangery, Kensington Palace

SPICED HOT CHOCOLATE

Although decidedly less time-consuming to prepare, this aromatic hot chocolate infused with cardamom, star anise, chilli and cinnamon is not dissimilar to the chocolate consumed at the English court during the seventeenth and eighteenth centuries (see pages 58–61). Melting dark chocolate into milk produces an intense cocoa hit – a far cry from stirring hot chocolate powder through boiled water.

Serves 4

the seeds from 2 cardamom pods, freshly ground

2 pods from a star anise

a pinch of chilli flakes

1 tsp ground cinnamon

grated zest of ½ orange

75g dark chocolate (minimum 70 per cent cocoa solids), broken into small pieces

400ml full-fat milk

Put the cardamom seeds and star anise into a frying pan and heat gently for 1–2 minutes to toast the spices. Stir in the chilli flakes, cinnamon and orange zest and continue to cook for another minute until the zest dries out a little.

Put into a mortar and use the pestle to grind the mixture into a fine powder.

Put the powder into a pan with the chocolate and milk and slowly bring to the boil, stirring well. Heat for a few minutes until the chocolate has all melted and the liquid is hot.

Divide among four small glasses and serve.

CHOCOLATE MOCKTAIL

This thick, creamy take on an after-dinner cocktail is decadently rich so it's best served after a light meal or as a pudding in its own right.

Serves 2

40ml maple syrup, plus a little extra for the rim

10g finely grated dark chocolate (minimum 70 per cent cocoa solids)

2 tbsp cocoa powder

1 egg yolk, at room temperature

2 tsp dark muscovado sugar

50ml coconut milk

50ml water

4 ice cubes

Brush a little maple syrup around the edge of two cocktail glasses. Sprinkle half the chopped chocolate on to a saucer. Dip the rim of each glass into it to coat then set aside to dry.

Put the cocoa powder into a cocktail shaker and add the egg yolk, maple syrup, sugar, coconut milk, water and ice cubes.

Shake well and strain equally between the two Martini glasses. Garnish with the remaining grated chocolate.

CHOCOLATE INTO
THE PRESENT DAY

By the time George III (r1760–1820) succeeded to the British throne in 1760, the position of royal chocolate maker was vacant – and the new king made no attempt to recruit. George was very afraid of the Hanoverian tendency to put on weight, and he adopted extremely frugal eating habits. Rich, luxurious chocolate was definitely not on the royal menu. Unlike his grandfather, George II, his preferred breakfast drink was not chocolate but 'unsweetened tea with hardly any milk in'. His wife Queen Charlotte also preferred tea to chocolate and was rarely seen without a teapot to hand.

George III was also under parliamentary pressure to cut spending. With wars to fight (and a family of 15 children to pay for), a chocolate maker was an obvious household expense to cull. Moreover, by the 1760s chocolate had become less exotic and exclusive. Tax and import duties were reduced, and England accrued more colonies suitable for producing chocolate, so it was in wider and cheaper supply.

The influence of the court was also waning as more powers transferred away from the king towards parliament. The court became associated with stuffy formality rather than glamorous luxury. Nonetheless, chocolate still featured in recipes and confectionery produced for royal consumption.

Although the chocolate enjoyed by the Stuart and Georgian royals was mostly drunk, there are early recipes for cakes and creams. Mary Eales, who claimed to be Queen Anne's confectioner, published her recipes for candied fruits and jams. Most tantalisingly, she includes a recipe for 'Chocolate almonds': half a pound of sugar and a pound of chocolate, perfumed with ambergris and musk, then sifted and shaped to look like almonds. Also included are macaroons, which she calls 'Chocolate puffs': three ounces of chocolate and half a pound of sugar are mixed together with 'White of Eggs whip'd to a Froth; then beat it well in a Mortar, and make it up in Loaves, or any Fashion you please. Bake it in a cool Oven, on Papers and Tin-Plates'.

The famous royal chef Marie-Antoine Carême, who cooked King George IV's (r1820–1830) most splendid banquets, included chocolate in his grand, hugely calorific concoctions and towering pastries. Carême, former chef to Napoleon, was possibly the greatest chef and patisserier of his age, most famous for his *pièces montées* – spun sugar and fondant sculptures that he displayed in the window of his Parisian patisserie. He was lured to work in England by George IV when he was Prince Regent and already notorious for his extravagant lifestyle and appetite. Carême pandered to his tastes, delighting his patron with fabulous, if health-threatening, rich and inventive dishes. At one particularly colossal state banquet in 1817 for the prince and his guest, the chef served nearly 200 sweet and savoury dishes. But possibly the highlights of the dinner were eight centrepieces, each some three feet in height. They were mainly made of spun sugar, fondant and marzipan, including a tower of caramelised profiteroles with pistachios and a pastry version of Brighton's Royal Pavilion! It was an era that represents the height of royal chocolate decadence.

The chocolate manufacturers of the twentieth century simultaneously found ways of making chocolate even cheaper by speeding up the processing and finding ways of using less cocoa. This same ingenuity brought with it a plethora of chocolate products: snack bars with wafers, layered with caramel and other fillings, shaped into eggs and filled with fondant. The most successful are now household names.

Perhaps as a reaction to the wide availability of inexpensive chocolate with low cocoa-solid content, in recent years the trend for luxury chocolate with exotic additions (sea salt, chilli, etc.) has flourished. The royal link still exists and although Her Majesty Queen Elizabeth II is not known for being as fixated on chocolate as some of her Georgian ancestors, a couple of luxury brands – Charbonnel et Walker and Bendicks – retain Royal Warrants and are proud to call themselves 'Chocolate Makers to the Queen'.

The early Mesoamerican nobles, the Spanish and the English royal courts all thought that chocolate was special. It was so expensive and delicious that it was thought of as a luxury associated with gift-giving and regal generosity. Echoing the Spanish *regalo* tradition, we still give chocolate as a token of love or of gratitude today. We bake it and drink it and cherish it as a mood-boosting treat, exactly as it has been enjoyed for thousands of years.

BOOZY CREAMY HOT CHOCOLATE

Many of the English monarchs are renowned for their love of excess. Queen Anne was chided by her doctor for her overindulgence in cakes and sweetmeats, while the lavish tastes of Edward VII, son of Victoria and Albert, are well documented. Though we're not advocating the cooked breakfast, 8-course lunch, high tea, lengthy dinner and the light supper taken just before bedtime that Edward enjoyed, there's no harm in spoiling ourselves once in a while. So savour every mouthful of this rum-laced hot chocolate topped with a healthy dollop of sweetened whipped cream. It's a sumptuous concoction, most certainly fit for every king and queen, despite what their doctor might say.

Serves 4

100g milk chocolate, broken into pieces

4 tbsp rum

a pinch of ground ginger, plus extra to sprinkle

400ml semi-skimmed milk

100–150ml double cream

1 tbsp icing sugar

Put the chocolate pieces in a heavy-based pan with the rum, ground ginger and milk. Place over a low heat to melt the chocolate slowly then gradually bring to the boil, whisking all the time until the mixture is smooth.

Whip the double cream in a bowl with the icing sugar until just thick.

Divide the hot chocolate among four glasses, then top with the double cream and a sprinkle of ground ginger.

HOT WHITE CHOCOLATE SAUCE

White chocolate is by far the sweetest of the three types of chocolate so this sauce needs something slightly tart to cut through its richness. Pour it over frozen summer berries, sharp grilled plums or stewed cooking apples for a quick and easy pudding.

Serves 4-6

3 egg yolks, at room temperature

2 tsp vanilla extract

150ml double cream

150ml full-fat milk

40g white chocolate, chopped

Put the egg yolks into a bowl and use a spatula to stir in the vanilla extract until the two ingredients are mixed together.

Pour the double cream and milk into a small pan and bring just to the boil. It's ready when bubbles start to appear around the edge of the liquid.

As soon as the cream mixture has just come to the boil, pour on to the egg yolk mixture. Stir well. Pour the mixture back into the pan and heat gently for 3 minutes to cook the eggs, stirring all the time. Take care not to overheat the pan or the mixture will overcook and scramble. The sauce is ready when it just coats the back of the spoon.

Stir in the white chocolate and heat through to melt, then pour into a warm jug and serve.

CHOCOLATE AND PEANUT SPREAD

Combining salty and sweet flavours is a time-honoured union and a true delight for the taste buds. If you're in need of further convincing think of cheese and chutney, honey and mustard ham, or turn to page 93 and bake a batch of Salted Caramel Brownies. Here the salty toasted peanuts perfectly balance the sweet milky chocolate, making this a moreish toast topping for any time of the day.

Makes around 300g

100g shelled peanuts

1 tsp salt

50ml coconut oil

1 tbsp cocoa powder

2 tbsp maple syrup

100g dark chocolate (minimum 50 per cent cocoa solids) broken into pieces

Sterilise a 350g jar and set aside.

Put the peanuts in a frying pan and cook over a low to medium heat for about 5 minutes until golden. Toss the peanuts every now and then to ensure they don't burn. Stir in the salt.

Transfer the peanuts and salt to a blender and pulse the mixture to grind down the nuts until they form a paste. Add the coconut oil, cocoa powder, maple syrup and chocolate and continue to whizz to combine. Check the paste is sweet enough for your taste or add a little more salt if it needs more seasoning, and whizz again to combine.

Spoon into a sterilised jar and seal. Once opened, store in the fridge and enjoy within two weeks.

Picture right: Fountain Court, Hampton Court Palace

HISTORIC ROYAL PALACES

Six palaces that span nearly a thousand years of history, with a myriad of treasures to share . . . Historic Royal Palaces is the independent charity that has in its charge six remarkable institutions: The Tower of London, Hampton Court Palace, Kensington Palace, Kew Palace, the Banqueting House and Hillsborough Castle, Northern Ireland. Each of the palaces in our care has survived for hundreds of years.

They have witnessed peace and prosperity and splendid periods of building and expansion but they also share stories of more turbulent times, of war and domestic strife, politics and revolution. These are places where history was made, by kings and queens, politicians and servants, rogues and rebels, craftsmen and traders, philosophers and philanderers, guards and gardeners. The palaces have witnessed strategy, intrigue, ambition, romance, devotion and disaster. World-changing events and the minutiae of everyday domestic life. The grand sweep, and the private moments.

Each palace is symbolic of Britain, and all have world significance. Once they were only for the privileged, now everyone can visit. We give these palaces continuing life. We welcome people, we stage events, we entertain. Our cause is to explore the stories of how monarchs and people shaped society, in some of the greatest palaces ever built. We warmly invite you to come and enjoy these fabulous buildings; to share their stories and to support us in our work, so that we can give the palaces a future as valuable as their past.

We offer an exciting programme of events and exhibitions throughout the year. Details on this, how to buy tickets and further information about visiting all the palaces can be found on our website. For more information please visit www.hrp.org.uk to discover our exciting programme of events and exhibitions throughout the year, plus how to buy tickets and full details of how to plan and enjoy your visit.

Visit our online store for our full range of beautiful gifts, including the turquoise and gold fine bone 'Royal Palace' china featured in this book, all inspired by centuries of stories from six amazing palaces.

TOWER OF LONDON

Gaze up at the massive White Tower, tiptoe through a king's medieval bedchamber and marvel at the Crown Jewels. Meet the Yeoman Warders with bloody tales to tell; stand where famous heads rolled and prisoners wept – then discover even more surprising stories about the Tower.

HAMPTON COURT PALACE

Explore Henry VIII's magnificent palace, then stroll through the elegant baroque apartments and glorious formal gardens of William III and Mary II. Feel the heat of the vast Tudor Kitchens and the eerie chill of the Haunted Gallery, before you disappear into the Maze, where whispers of the past will haunt every step to the centre of this topiary puzzle.

BANQUETING HOUSE

Walk in the footsteps of a dazzling company of courtiers who once danced, drank and partied beneath the magnificent Rubens-painted ceiling. This revolutionary building was created for court entertainments, but is probably most famous for the execution of Charles I in 1649. Spare him a thought as you gaze up at this ravishing painting – one of his last sights on Earth.

KEW PALACE (OPEN APRIL-SEPTEMBER)

Step inside this tiny doll's house of a palace and sense the joys and sorrows of past royal lives in intimate detail, as King George III and his family come to life through a radio play and display of fascinating personal artefacts. Experience a riot of colour in authentically re-created Georgian rooms, before wandering through the eerie rooms of the upper floor, left untouched for centuries.

Stroll to Queen Charlotte's cottage, built in 1770, where the royal family enjoyed picnics and peace in a tranquil corner of Kew Gardens. Don't miss the tours of the atmospheric Royal Kitchens – an experience to savour. Re-opened in 2012 and presented 'as found', this rare Georgian survival will spark your imagination as you sense the presence of the people who prepared, cooked and served food for the royal household, almost 200 years ago.

KENSINGTON PALACE

Take the journey of a courtier through the splendid King's Apartments and marvel at the impressive rooms and the wall and ceiling paintings. Or discover the private and personal secrets revealed with the Queen's State Apartments. Tempted by some more recent glamour? You'll love the stylish displays celebrating modern royals, including Princess Diana. Or explore the life, loves, triumphs and tragedies of Queen Victoria, from lonely princess to her final years, before enjoying a delicious cream tea in the elegant Orangery.

HILLSBOROUGH CASTLE (OPEN APRIL–SEPTEMBER)

This elegant Georgian mansion, with its beautiful gardens, holds a unique place in the recent history of Northern Ireland, having served as a venue for both the formal and informal stages of the peace process. It came under the management of Historic Royal Palaces in April 2014. Built in the late eighteenth century by Wills Hill, First Marquis of Downshire, Hillsborough was the principal seat for the Downshires for over 100 years until it passed into public ownership. It became an official royal residence in 1920, and members of the royal family have visited regularly since 1922.

Picture right: Tower of London

INDEX

Historic Royal Palaces is an independent charity. We raise all our own funds and depend on the support of our visitors, members, donors, sponsors and volunteers. The proceeds from the sale of *Chocolate Fit For A Queen*, as do all our gifts and merchandise, go to support our work, so thank you for buying this book and helping to maintain the beautiful historic buildings for future generations to enjoy.

We would like to thank Carey Smith and Lydia Good at Ebury and the creative team who produced the book: Jan Baldwin, Imogen Fortes, Tabitha Hawkins and Emma Marsden, as well as Alareen Farrell and Sarah Kilby at Historic Royal Palaces.

1 3 5 7 9 10 8 6 4 2

Published in 2015 by Ebury Press, an imprint of Ebury Publishing

Ebury Press is part of the Penguin Random House group of companies whose
addresses can be found at global.penguinrandomhouse.com

Text © Historic Royal Palaces 2015
Layout and design © Ebury Press 2015

Picture credits:
All food photography by Jan Baldwin
All other photography by Historic Royal Palaces

The turquoise and gold fine bone china 'Royal Palace' tea set featured in some of
the photographs is exclusive to Historic Royal Palaces, and is available from their
online shop www.hrp.rg.uk.

A CIP catalogue record for this book is available from the British Library

The Random House Group Limited supports the Forset Stewardship Council® (FSC®),
the leading international forest-certification organisation. Our books carrying the FSC
label are printed on FSC®-certified paper. FSC is the only forest-certification scheme
supported by the leading environmental organisations, including Greenpeace. Our
paper procurement policy can be found at: www.randomhouse.co.uk/environment

MIX
Paper from
responsible sources
FSC® C008047

To buy books by your favourite authors and register for offers visit
www.randomhouse.co.uk

Text written by Polly Putnam, Collections Curator, Historic Royal Palaces;
adapted from her original research into the Chocolate Kitchens at Hampton
Court Palace.
Editor for Historic Royal Palaces: Sarah Kilby
Recipes and food styling: Emma Marsden
Photographer: Jan Baldwin
Prop styling and art direction: Tabitha Hawkins
Project editor: Imogen Fortes
Copyeditor: Julia Kellaway
Typesetter: Akihiro Nakayama
Cover Design: Akihiro Nakayama

Printed and bound in China by C&C Offset Printing Co., Ltd
ISBN 9781785031243